Symbolism

Translated from the Dutch by Leonard Scott

Symbolism

by Bettina Spaanstra-Polak

J. M. Meulenhoff Amsterdam 1967

Art and architecture in the Netherlands

already published:

J. B. Jongkind / John Raedecker / Neo-realism in Painting / The
'De Stijl' Group / The Experimentalists / Herman Kruyder / Van
Dongen / Jaap Wagemaker / Jaap Nanninga / Lucebert / Mari An-
driessen / Kees Verwey / Henri ten Holt / Jan Sluijters / Constant /
Domela / André Volten / Geertgen tot Sint Jans / Gerrit Benner /
Hendrik Chabot / Wessel Couzijn / J. J. P. Oud / K. P. C. de Bazel

in preparation:

G. H. Breitner / Corneille / The Expressionists / Edgar Fernhout /
Isaac Israels / Hercules Seghers / H. P. Berlage / B. Merkelbach
L. C. van der Vlugt

A series of works on art and architecture in the Netherlands
edited by:
R. Blijstra / D. Dooijes / B. J. E. M. de Hoog / J. Hulsker / H. L. C.
Jaffé / A. B. de Vries

Introduction

One of the most characteristic expressions of artistic creativeness towards the end of the nineteenth century is symbolism. We meet it in the visual arts, and even earlier in literature. It was not limited to a few countries but was to be found all over Europe. In the Netherlands symbolism played an important part in the work of a small group of artists, and this factor was to exert its influence on the course of art in the twentieth century.

Before going on to explain the content of symbolism, let us outline the circumstances in which the movement originated and flourished.

After the French Revolution, at the beginning of the nineteenth century, the relationship between artist and patron and between artist and society underwent a radical change. Instead of Church and State – pope and emperor, prelates and patricians – there appeared after Napoleon a new patron of the arts: the free burghers, the middle classes. But these had not grown up in the tradition of patronage of former times, so that the artist was no longer sure of his bread and butter. Criticism in the rapidly developing daily press was another new factor for the artist to reckon with. And yet another was the regular holding of exhibitions which had come into fashion since Napoleon. For the first time in history commoners were free to visit museums and exhibition halls, learn to appreciate works of art and make a critical choice. One of the results of this was that certain artists who failed to satisfy popular taste and gain official recognition felt themselves misunderstood and neglected, and began to organize their own exhibitions. Examples of this are the *Salon des Refusés* of the Paris impressionists (where in 1863 Manet exhibited his *Déjeuner sur l'herbe*), the avant-garde *Société des XX*, founded in Brussels in 1884, and the *Haagse Kunstkring* of 1891. The conflict between the artist and the average citizen, who did not understand him, came out sharply in the Romantic Period. By the end of the nineteenth century the chasm had become unbridgeable.

Apart from the French Revolution, the industrial revolution too was of profound importance. The mechanically produced factory article was cheaper than the product of artistic skill and started to replace it. There arose an antithesis between the artist, who painted expensive pictures for the better class of well-to-do citizen, and the craftsman. 'Arts and crafts' became the vogue in the nineteenth century. Estrangement from society and the rise of the arts and crafts movement were a severe blow for the artist. His reaction was twofold. On the one hand he was inclined to sever all ties with society and to take refuge in an ivory tower, there to create 'art for art's sake'. This gave us the bohemian type, the dandy, whose attitude was a provocation hurled at society, a conscious desire to shock. The prime example was Oscar Wilde.

On the other hand we find the socially directed attitude: the artist wanted to re-establish his ties with society and take up his former position again. A distinctive feature of this attitude was a nostalgic longing for a better social order, such as was imagined to have existed in the Middle Ages, in which the individual worked in the guilds under the inspiration of an all-embracing faith. In mid-nineteenth-century England this nostalgia was evident in the Pre-Raphaelite Brotherhood, in Dante Gabriel Rossetti, John Everett Millais, William Holman Hunt, and at the end of the century in Holland in Antoon Derkinderen. Others who cherished similar ideals in England were John Ruskin and William Morris. They fiercely attacked ugly industrial products, urging that the artist should at the same time be a craftsman, that he should not only design furniture, wallpaper, and so on, but also produce them. The artist-craftsman should take delight in his work; he should not put his talent at the service of some rich individual but should make it available to the community as a whole. The Belgian architect Henry van de Velde adopted these ideals and became an advocate, in lectures and in his writings, of the union of beauty and art in the service of the community. However, van de Velde looked upon mass production not as something to be rejected but as an extremely useful tool at the disposal of applied art.

The ideal demanding that the artist should work for the community as both designer and creator was also championed by Walter Crane in 1892 in his *The Claims of Decorative Art*. Its translation into Dutch by Jan Veth under the title *Kunst en Samenleving* two years later had a great influence on artistic ideals in Holland, especially on the idea of 'community art', more or less tinged with socialism.

It was not only their changed social position that affected artists: the struggle between the propertied class and the rising industrial proletariat, the struggle between capitalism and socialism also had an influence on them. Depending on their individual make-up, they reacted to the poignant contrast between wealth and poverty by turning either to socialism or to anarchism. The less militant spirits fled to the higher spheres of religion or to the vaguer domains of mysticism, which they usually found in Roman Catholicism or such Eastern religions as Buddhism. They also sought help in occultism, spiritualism, black magic and theosophy, or in such syncretic teachings as those of the Rosicrucians. This order gained a new lease of life in Paris in 1888 through the activities of Sar Joséphin Péladan, who in his highly personal bombastic writings raised the artist to the rank of priest and hoped to save mankind from materialism through the mysticism of the Holy Grail and Richard Wagner's music dramas. In 1892, at the same time as Paul Verlaine, Péladan made a trip to the Netherlands, dressed up as a magus in a black astrakhan hat, a purple silk blouse, a long cape and top boots.

Their isolated position in society drove the artists together for safety. Nationally and internationally, contacts were maintained on a large scale. Poets and painters visited each other, gave banquets for one another and kept up a lively correspondence. International contact was also kept up in the weeklies and magazines, which were excellently informed of all the doings of artists at home and abroad.

To sum up, we may say that all these factors were conducive to a powerful individualism. The artist's urge to give expression to what was going on inside him, his need to lay bare his own experiences of life and his own outlook upon life, gave rise to the movement we know as symbolism.

Symbolism as a Phenomenon

To avoid any misunderstanding, we must make a clear distinction between two different meanings of the word symbolism. It is used in a general sense to mean the practice or art of using symbols. For example, the symbolism of the colour red in the liturgy of the Roman Catholic Church is love, purple stands for penance or mourning, white is for purity.

In addition to this general use of the term, symbolism also refers to a *historical* phenomenon or movement that had distinct origins in about 1885, a culminating point in the years 1892 and 1893, and by 1900 was a thing of the past. In both literature and the visual arts this movement had certain definite features. The word *symboliste* occurred for the first time in a French manifesto published in 1886, in which the poet Jean Moréas, of Greek origin, described the object of poetry in these terms: to express ideas and emotions in concrete form by the free use of words and sounds, of style and rhythm; words should not be uttered or apprehended clearly but should stimulate the imagination of the reader by their mysterious and enigmatic character; the word should acquire magic power, evoke images, suggest rather than state. This manifesto had already been put into practice by the poets Mallarmé, Rimbaud and Verlaine and by novelists such as Joris-Karl Huysmans, who had tried to communicate their most personal fantasies, their most intimate promptings by the evocative power of words. Generally speaking, what they wanted was more mysticism, more illusion, more music.

In the Netherlands the literary movement of the 1880s might be termed symbolist. The poet Willem Kloos declared in 1890 that art 'should be the most individual expression of the most individual emotion'.

The most distinctive aspect of symbolism is of course its symbols:

both in literature and in art, they keep recurring with greater or lesser intensity, and no matter whether they are written or painted, they are always the same.

Nevertheless, the symbol as used by the symbolists is always pregnant with meaning, suggestive of a highly personal world of feelings and ideas. These symbols are not new: they were already known in the Middle Ages and the Renaissance. But in those days they were used in a general way, as allegories, as universal truths revealing nothing of the individual emotions of the artist. For the spirit of the age was such that artists chose to depict traditional subjects from the Bible, mythology and allegory. However, with the emergence of the Romantic Period, when the artist no longer worked exclusively for the Church and his prince but was thrown back upon himself, he naturally turned to subjects relating to his own environment, his own existence. He no longer sees nature as mere scenery, however pretty, but as a reflection of his inner life. Trees are humanized, looked upon as animated beings; and the artist sees himself mirrored in the sea.

Woman, hitherto represented as a muse, a goddess, a nymph or a charming piece of decoration, becomes the principal subject of the artist, now that he has learnt to see her as an individual and recognized her in the most personal experiences – in young love, in the sufferings of love, in marriage, in an unhappy marriage, as an adulteress, courtesan or prostitute.

Every representation of Woman – be it in poetry, prose, painting, drawing or sculpture – becomes a crystallization, that is to say the confession of an experience undergone by the artist himself. Woman, capable of rousing the most base and the most noble emotions in man, is still seen in the light of the unjust, one-sided morality of the period. Married life, in which at first she plays the part of the inferior, but after her emancipation more the equal of her husband, constitutes one of the major themes of nineteenth-century art. In literature, examples spring immediately to mind. Flaubert's *Madame Bovary* became world-famous because it was the first novel to deal with what had always been a taboo subject: the unhappy wife who takes a lover. In Tolstoy's *Anna Karenina* and D. H. Lawrence's *Lady Chatterley's Lover* the same problem is treated from a psychological angle. Before Sigmund Freud freed eroticism and sexuality from spurious and sanctimonious morality and published his epoch-making writings, his life's work had as it were already been heralded in the literature and the painting of the *fin de siècle*, in the symbols of the symbolists.

The unshakable, hypocritical middle-class morality – which held that everything pertaining to the spiritual life, to the soul, was on a higher plane than the world of the senses and the animal instincts – led to an extreme repression of natural urges. This morality was particularly dominant in the second half of the nineteenth century, in the Victorian era. And repression sought an outlet in sharp contrasts of sensuality and continence, of voluptuousness and asceticism.

Earthly pleasures were looked upon as sins, with which the higher aspirations of the soul were utterly incompatible. An irreconcilable discord between matter and mind revealed itself most glaringly in relations between the sexes. In the current attitudes of Christianity and Marxism we find the same contrast, and it is by no means impossible that the renewed influence of Neo-Platonism intensified this notion that there is a higher world of the spirit and a lower world of the senses in the consciousness of the period. All symbolist literature – and painting too – is permeated by this opposition, stated in terms of black and white, between body and mind, sin and chastity. Richard Wagner's music dramas *Parsifal* and *Lohengrin*, Maeterlinck's plays (*Pelléas et Mélisande*, for instance) and the paintings of the Pre-Raphaelites enjoyed overwhelming success in the closing decades of the nineteenth century by mingling these two elements, though as yet they were veiled in Grail mysticism, Norse legend and Arthurian romance.

In painting, this period was the first in which married life was represented as a personal experience rather than in general allegorical terms. The Norwegian Edvard Munch gives us examples in such works as *Ashes, Separation, Jealousy* and *The Dance of Life*. And so do Ibsen and Strindberg in their plays. In Holland Jan Toorop introduced a sensual element into practically all his symbolist work – for instance, in his *Rôdeurs*, where lustful male hands stretch out towards an innocent young girl (Plate II).

Between 1890 and 1900, mainly under Wagner's influence, the theme of sensuality radiated such obsessive power that artists and writers in France, the Netherlands and Norway, independently of each other, gave shape to the same feelings and thoughts.

The Symbols
The constantly recurring symbols of this movement give expression to what is most essential to the artist: relations between the sexes, his outlook on life, thoughts of destiny and death, his inward self and his position in society. The *femme fatale*, source of inspiration to the romantics and still more to the symbolists, is the most important symbol. She is the primordial seductress, seeking material gain and the ruin of men. She lures her prey with her long, flowing, luxuriant hair and large, venomous green eyes. The symbolists found these characteristics of the *femme fatale* embodied in a few female types: Salome, Cleopatra, Medusa and the Sphinx.

With Salome, stress is laid on the oriental elegance and exotic splendour she exhibits in her dance before King Herod. The reward she demands is the head of John the Baptist. This mixture of lasciviousness and sadism reaches a peak of originality in Oscar Wilde's *Salomé*, written in French in 1891, which would have been performed in Paris, with Sarah Bernhardt in the title role, if the censor had not stepped in and banned the performance. Wilde's play, which was finally put on in Paris in 1896, was famed for Aubrey Beardsley's black-and-white illustrations for the English edition of 1894, especially the scene in which Herod's unnatural daughter raises the blood-stained head of John the Baptist and kisses it (Plate 30). This theme, repeatedly imitated by poets and illustrators, also inspired the Dutchman Henricus (Plate 31). In music too we meet Salome. In 1901 Massenet's opera *Hérodiade*, composed in 1881, was performed in Dordrecht. In 1905 Richard Strauss immortalized Salome a second time, in the music drama in which Salome dances the sultry dance of the seven veils.

Cleopatra is represented as a ravishing, enigmatic beauty, reclining on her couch under a starry sky on the banks of the Nile, surrounded by luxury, decked in all kinds of gems. Like Salome, she is cruel and alluring. The serpent and the scarab (a turquoise-coloured Egyptian beetle) are her attributes.

In Greek mythology, the once beautiful Medusa, with her head now covered with snakes instead of hair and her huge staring eyes that turned mortals to stone, was decapitated by Perseus. Her pale, stony face with its soulless, fixed stare had fascinated such poets of Romanticism as Goethe, Keats and Shelley. The symbolists too came under her spell: in Medusa's head they discovered beauty and destruction, desire and suffering. The painters represent her as a satanic monster with the face of a Greek goddess, a ghostly mask whose most sinister feature is its pupil-less eyes that cannot see or weep or even flicker.

Of outstanding significance for the *fin de siècle* was the Sphinx. In the first place, she was the symbol of Woman – evil, seductive, enigmatic, the one that poses the riddle of life. But she is also the symbol of the riddle of life itself. She stands for all that is mysterious in the universe, in nature and particularly in human life. According to Greek mythology the Sphinx, which lived at the gates of Thebes, had a woman's head, the body of a lion, the claws and wings of a bird. She let no man pass who could not solve the riddle: 'What is it that has one voice and yet becomes four-footed and two-footed and three-footed?' The unfortunates who did not know the answer were hurled into the abyss. Oedipus, however, gave the right answer: Man, who crawls on all fours in infancy, stands erect on two feet in manhood and leans on a staff in old age. The Sphinx thereupon threw herself down into the abyss. To the adherents of occultism and spiritualism the Sphinx became a favourite emblem. A magazine of this name was published in Germany, and in the heyday of symbolism, 1893–1895, in the Netherlands too. In prose and poetry the Sphinx appears on countless occasions. She was the subject of paintings by Fernand Khnopff in Belgium and by Toorop in Holland (Cover, plates 4 and 13).

As old as the account of the Creation, and always connected with Woman – the Serpent is for the symbolists no longer the accomplice of Woman but the very symbol of her who has become at once snake and she-devil. Like the Sphinx, the Serpent evokes the corrupt enchantment of the forbidden act. Other symbols of evil are the Chimaera, a monster with a lion's head, goat's body and serpent's tail, and the Harpy, a mythological creature with a woman's face and the claws of a beast of prey, like the vulture a symbol of cruelty and rapacity, ever ready to swoop down on human beings as soon as they weaken in their defence (Plate 5).

The antagonist of the *femme fatale* is Pan. This satyr with his goat's feet and horns, in antiquity the god of forests and shepherds, was to become towards the close of the nineteenth century, because of his exuberant zest for life, the symbol of virile erotic passion. With his grinning, voluptuous mask, derisive of bourgeois morality and hypocrisy, he also became the symbol in a broader sense of a rejuvenated feeling for life and new ideas. This is why his name was chosen for a magazine, founded in Berlin in 1895, devoted to modern art and literature. No poem was complete without its Pan, with his pipes, frolicking in the rushes or chasing the nymphs, or languidly rolling about on a warm summer's day. Mallarmé's poem *L'après-midi d'un faune*, dating from 1876, inspired Claude Debussy in 1892 to compose one of his most exquisite orchestral pieces.

Pan's brother is the mythological centaur, whose body turns at the hips into the trunk of a horse. In 1896 there appeared in Paris a periodical named *Le Centaure* after him.

As white contrasts with black, and good with evil, the innocent young woman was the opposite of the *femme fatale*. A symbol of innocence and purity, she was to the symbolists the visionary ideal of otherworldly, spiritual love. As the object of veneration and adoration from afar on the model of the mystic love which the medieval young man was supposed to have entertained for his lady – for instance, Dante's love for Beatrice – she became a hazy, transparent being. She was transformed into the vision seen in a dream (symbol of innocence *par excellence*). And the young girls of the nineteenth century were educated to this world of illusion, that is to say in absolute ignorance of natural life and the dark dominion of sexuality.

The bride was looked upon as the purest symbol of female chastity and purity. For she who is on the point of entering into matrimony and consequently of losing her virginal innocence is on this day of rejoicing still the symbol of innocence. A variant of the bride motif is Mélisande in Maeterlinck's drama *Pelléas et Mélisande* (1892), which thoroughly entranced *fin de siècle* Europe, especially after Debussy had set it to music. Mélisande, who had conceived a chaste, almost sisterly love for her brother-in-law Pelléas, was seen as a fairy with long blonde hair that fell about her shoulders like a cloak.

The attributes of the innocent young woman were the flower symbols—lily, iris, rose, sunflower, lotus—and also the noble swan. This popular creature of the Celtic Middle Ages was not only the mystic helper of Lohengrin, who inWagner's music drama arrives in a boat, drawn by a swan, to save Elsa of Brabant; it was also a symbol of the purity of the soul.

It is easily understood that the symbolists, with their sensitivity to the sound and rhythm of free verse and their appreciation of music in general, should choose musical instruments as symbols: the harp, the lyre, the violin, the piano and the organ. Played by woman's hands, they interpret a scale of emotions ranging from sorrow to the utmost bliss (Plates 20 and 21).

The theme of Fate was almost as important as that of the Sphinx. He who saw no way out of calamity, who felt doomed through heredity, was in the grip of Fate. Where Fate has once struck, beauty and love can never return. After Edgar Allan Poe in his famous poem *The Raven*, in 1845, gave voice to the notion of fatality, condensed in the word 'nevermore' issuing from the raven's beak, Poe was adopted by the symbolists. His 'nevermore' echoed through the poetry of the whole of Europe. In painting, Fate was symbolized in the actual figure of the chained Prometheus or by an ironclad fist pressing down heavy as lead on a shackled figure, reminiscent again of Prometheus in his chains.

On the heels of Fate comes Death. If for the romantics Death could still be either a dread visitation or a comforting friend, to the symbolists Death had become the demoniacal destructive force in the shape of a skeleton, the King of Terrors, or of a grim old witch. Death was also bound up with beauty and debauchery. In symbolist literature the murderer has a peculiar sensation of lust when he looks at the beauty he has killed. In painting, particularly in Toorop's work, death's-heads and churchyards appear in conjunction with a beautiful young woman (Plate II).

Since one of the most essential characteristics of the symbolists was the revelation of personal emotions, the world of the soul became one of their preferred themes. The word 'soul' appeared time and again. The world of the soul not only contains grief and pain, which chasten the human spirit, but also solitude, desolation, despair and moods of melancholy and boredom (spleen), of autumn and twilight. Personal grief and isolation were also expressed in the image of Him whose sufferings exceeded all human experience – in identification with Christ. The word God was used to give full emphasis to personal emotion, but this was no indication of any Christian religious conviction.

We could certainly fill out our catalogue of symbols with the Present, the Past and the Future, the Young Girl, the Mature Woman and the Old Woman, Anarchy and Labour, together with the Sower, but our intention was to give no more than an outline of the most important symbols, without aiming at completeness.

Symbolism in Painting
About 1890 – later than in literature – symbolism manifests itself in painting throughout Europe, but again with France as its birthplace.

Painters, who felt the need to give expression to their feelings of love, hatred, pessimism or grief, and to their whole attitude to life, were no longer satisfied with the technique of impressionism with its surprising light effects and nuances. It is no longer their purpose to depict the familiar image of reality observed in terms of space and depth, local colour, special lighting or the individual impression created by man or animal. They want only to reveal what is going on in their hearts in a straightforward, evocative formal language – preferably charged with magical power.

In consequence, the rich variety of the colourful palette gives way to a simplified method of painting, a more concise statement in outline, filled in with colour, and finally a linear stylization without any colour at all. The painting thus becomes a drawing. Its individual and temporary nature becomes universally valid and timeless. Three-dimensional representation is ousted by two-dimensional, decorative, flat indication. The flat surface filled with line and colour is what remains.

This simplified type of composition appeared for the first time about 1888 in a painting by Paul Gauguin, showing a landscape in which Breton peasant women are outlined figures filled in with colour. Gauguin had a great influence on the painters who worked with him in Brittany (Pont-Aven and Le Pouldu). The same new style was also applied by the *Nabis* (the 'prophets' or 'leaders'), who were in close contact with the Paris Rosicrucians and spiritualists. Members of this group included Vuillard, Bonnard and Maurice Denis. The latter succinctly formulated the nature of the new style in 1890, when he said that 'a picture – before being a warhorse, a nude or an anecdote of some sort – is essentially a flat surface covered with colours assembled in a certain order'.

Line and colour, which formerly served as means of depicting the subject, now acquired their own aesthetic or symbolic significance. The line became the most important element. The symbolist painters instilled such fierce energy into it that stylization went beyond all proportion and became distortion. This we see in the work of the English illustrator Aubrey Beardsley, the Austrian painter Gustav Klimt – and the Dutch symbolists in particular. Other features of the new composition are the emphasis on women's hair and on their eyes – which are large and misty or dark and hypnotic in their intensity (Plate 4) – and the technique of filling up the space between figures and background with a pattern of parallel lines which occasionally remind us of the grain in a piece of wood (Plates 8 and 17). The transition from impressionism to linear stylization was a gradual process. Because the symbolists wanted to express themselves as meaningfully as possible by means of the stylizing and distorting line, they were visually susceptible to the linear element they observed in the art of the remote and recent past. Sources of inspiration included medieval illuminated Bibles, paintings from the fifteenth and sixteenth centuries, Flemish, German and Italian painters like Memlinck, Albrecht Dürer, Hans Holbein the Younger, Botticelli, and so on.

And then there were the visions of William Blake at the beginning of the nineteenth century, and the pictures of the Pre-Raphaelites in mid-century. Particular inspiration was found in Japanese and Chinese lacquers and embroidery and Japanese prints with their delicate linear curves and almost total lack of perspective. This Oriental art, which had an influence on the development of the new manner in the applied arts (*Jugendstil* or Art Nouveau), was also of great importance to its development in the flat plane. It was partly due to the stylization and distortion of the symbolists that Art Nouveau took root in painting and the graphic arts, and this style became a major medium of expression for them.

Symbolism in Dutch Painting
In the Netherlands the rise of the symbolist movement in painting was closely linked with the literary movement of the eighties and nineties. Just as in Paris, Brussels and London there were strong ties between artists and writers, in Amsterdam, The Hague, the Gooi district (close to Amsterdam, with the towns of Laren, Hilversum and Bussum), and in Noordwijk and Katwijk, the poets and other writers, who also edited or contributed to the leading literary magazines, such as *De Nieuwe Gids* (1885) and P. L. Tak's *De Kroniek* (1895), were always in close contact with the painters, among whom we find the major symbolists.
Their connection with such poets as Willem Kloos, the idol of the eighties and nineties, Albert Verwey, Herman Gorter, and with the prose writers Lodewijk van Deyssel en Frederik van Eeden, greatly contributed to the tendency among the painters influenced by symbolism, especially Jan Toorop, R. N. Roland Holst and to a lesser extent Johan Thorn Prikker, to select and elaborate

themes they had found in the works of their literary friends. Literature came first, symbolist painting followed its lead. The latter started about 1890 and reached its peak in 1892 and 1893, to lose power gradually after 1894, until by the end of the century it had more or less disappeared.

Important meeting places, where there was a lively exchange of ideas and news of what was going on in the artistic world, were the cafés (such as Mast and Bodega in Amsterdam), the *Haagse Kunstkring* (founded in 1891 by Jan Toorop and others), the *Rotterdamsche Kunstkring* (1893), the *Arti et Amicitiae* building at the corner of Spui and Rokin in Amsterdam, and the large Panorama Building in the Plantage in Amsterdam.

Many of the great events in the world of art, for instance those that took place in the year 1892, were organized by the symbolists. In May 1892 the *Haagse Kunstkring* was host to the first Dutch exhibition of paintings and drawings by Vincent van Gogh, who had died in such tragic circumstances in 1890, and in December of the same year this exhibition moved to Amsterdam. In June and July there was a large Exhibition of Contemporary Dutch Painting in *Arti et Amicitiae* on the occasion of the anniversary celebrations of the Amsterdam student body. That same summer the *Haagse Kunstkring* organized a show of works by members of the Brussels *Société des XX* (who had first exhibited in Holland in the hall of the Panorama Building in Amsterdam in 1889). In November 1892 Paul Verlaine and the grand master of the French Rosicrucians Sar Péladan were fêted in Amsterdam, Leiden and The Hague, where they both gave lectures.

A fascinating picture of this stirring period and of all these artists with their friendships and quarrels is provided by the vast store of correspondence that has come down to us. In those days they took up the pen as easily as we pick up the telephone now! Much of this correspondence is preserved in the Literary Museum and the Royal Library in The Hague. We also gain interesting impressions from the memoirs of contemporaries or from the more recently published reminiscences of those of their friends or relations who are still living.

The two facets of the *fin de siècle* – mysticism and socialism – were also prominent in the art of the Dutch symbolist painters. A hothouse atmosphere (of which we have a psychologically magnificent picture in Louis Couperus's novel *Eline Vere*, 1889), a morbid revelling in daydreams and wishful thinking, in sadism and perversion, an inclination towards the mysterious, the exalted, the vague which passes for spirituality, a flying from reality into mysticism: all this we discover in the symbolism of Jan Toorop and Johan Thorn Prikker and a number of artists whom they influenced. To express their view of life and their personal confessions (represented by symbols) they endeavoured to find a formalized language, charged with magical power, which was to be universally valid.

This was the result: the spatial element in the picture undergoes a change, perspective disappears, and we are left with the flat surface. The forms may vary from neo-impressionism to Art Nouveau Symbolism is the content, Art Nouveau the form in which the symbols are communicated.

The consequences of these utterly personal communications, occasionally presented in the shape of the worst imaginable distortion, led finally to an incomprehensible secret language. Neither in its content nor in its form could this be understood by anyone but the artist himself.

Among the painters who for varying lengths of time came under the spell of symbolism, especially Toorop's symbolism, and were fascinated by Edgar Allan Poe's horror stories and the nightmarish scenes and apparitions produced by the French painter Odilon Redon, were Etienne Bosch, H. A. van Daalhoff, S. Moulijn, Floris Verster and particularly Henricus (pseudonym of Hendricus Jansen) (Plate 31), and towards 1900 P. C. de Moor, Antoon van Welie and Karel de Nerée tot Babberich (the Dutch Aubrey Beardsley).

Socialism, in the Netherlands militant and fiercely idealistic in its struggle for more social justice, revealed itself in the aspirations of Antoon Derkinderen and Richard Nicolaüs Roland Holst. With them, however, symbolism was only a passing phase. It was a kind of transitional stage, a means helping them in their search, right through and beyond reality, for the abstract – leading eventually to 'community art'. In the 1890s this was understood as a sort of amalgamation, the unification of painting (murals) with architecture and the applied arts (book production, ceramics, interior decoration and 'arts and crafts') under the name 'decorative art'.

According to Derkinderen and Roland Holst the function of the artist, who at the same time was a craftsman, was that of the priest – to disseminate his ideas among the people, the community. Art should be the servant of the whole of society and no longer of individual persons. Not beauty but ethics played the important part in this aspiration.

What characterizes the symbolist work of Derkinderen and Roland Holst is the almost total absence of distortion: what we find is a proportioned linear stylization in the surface pattern. After 1894 they exercised great influence on a group of decorative artists and illustrators of books, calendars and magazines such as G.W. Dijsselhof, C. A. Lion Cachet, Th. Nieuwenhuis, Th. van Hoytema and L. W. R. Wenckebach, on the ceramic designer Th. A. C. Colenbrander, and on the architects H. P. Berlage and K. P. C. de Bazel. Typical of their work too was ornamentation with flower, plant and animal motifs which were stylized and reshaped on the flat surface of the painting into two-dimensional forms. Towards 1900 these natural forms became more and more emaciated and rigid; occasionally they were interspersed with female figures that had become purely ornamental and are almost entirely lacking in symbolistic power. Eventually their ornamentation became absolutely symmetrical and geometric – the typical feature of the *Nieuwe Kunst* (the Dutch equivalent of Art Nouveau) – partly because of the philosophy of life of these artists, coloured as it was by ethics, theosophy and Calvinism. This *Nieuwe Kunst* – which in its severely geometric structure certainly forms a contrast with Art Nouveau outside Holland, so luxurious with its curving and twirly lines, though born of the same will to renew style and form – influenced industrial design well into the twentieth century.

Jan Theodoor Toorop (1858–1928)

Toorop was the most outstanding of Dutch symbolists. His partly Oriental descent (his father had Norwegian, his mother Chinese blood), his great talent for drawing (already evident when he was young), his musicality and his ardent interest in all that was happening in the world, and particularly in the world of literature – all this made him a compelling figure.

After leaving the country of his birth, Java, at an early age to settle in Holland, he went to Brussels in 1882 on a scholarship to the Academy of Fine Arts. His stay in Brussels was particularly important to his life as a man and as an artist. In 1885 he became a member of the *Société des XX*, founded the year before, and made friends with his fellow-members, thus establishing contacts that were to last for life with the Belgian painters James Ensor, Henry van de Velde (better known as an architect) and Fernand Khnopff. Returning to Holland for good in 1890, he painted one of his first symbolist pictures in Katwijk: *The Venus of the Sea* (Plate I). Toorop mixes observed reality – the Katwijk fisherman with his wife, the dunes and the sea – with fantasy – exotic shrubs, a baby and the Serpent from the Garden of Eden, and in their midst the *femme fatale* with her easy elegance (also reminiscent of Ibsen's drama *The Lady from the Sea*). She is there to work mischief and bring man to ruin. Toorop is obsessed by this theme; time after time it returns. Under the influence of Maeterlinck's dramas, in which the trees are animated beings, a change takes place in the background of Toorop's paintings. With chalk and pencil he draws gloomy scenes of ghostly gardens with dark ponds, overshadowed by weeping willows like living beings whose arms writhe like tentacles. From the branches women's hair streams down. In such a *Garden of Woes* death's-heads grow on thorns (Plate 2) – symbol of the destruction caused by lust. The churchyard – background to the sordid seducers of innocence, the *Rô-deurs*, offering trinkets to entice the girl, resting on her purple rug – makes its appearance again as the stage-setting for Death (Plate II).

We find demigod figures, like Javanese wayang puppets, appearing in Toorop's work after 1892; as a rule they are symbols of good and release the dead soul from its thorns and worldly passions (Plate 3). Space is steadily diminished, and linear stylization, full of symbolic power, undulates over the surface of the picture. In *The Three Brides*, 1893 (Plate III) – showing the innocent bride flanked by the ascetic non-bride and the 'infernal bride', the latter a kind of Cleopatra, holding in her hands a dish full of the blood of the victims of sensuality – the lines have their own symbolic meaning: in the evil bride the lines are sharply etched (Toorop himself called them 'gil- en pang-lijnen' – yell and bang lines); in the good bride the lines are soft and curved.

Finally, the lines in parallel strands predominate over the human figures to such an extent that they overflow into the frames and start living a life of their own, as in *The Song of the Times* (Plate 7). Here the anarchist makes his appearance, with hair like faggots, a motif that Toorop met in Carlyle's *On Heroes, Hero-Worship, and the Heroic in History*. He is the revolutionary leader, the barbarian breaking in two the yoke of Church and State or putting the two powers to flight (Plate 6). He is as evil a figure as the Sphinx. The Sphinx is either kept in check by a noble figure of a man or is herself tyrannizing her victims. The noble creatures who are not bowed down under her claws have a share in a better life, in mysticism (Plate 5).

In 1894 Toorop was under the spell of Wagner's and César Franck's music, and at the same time he was again stylistically inspired by William Blake. Wagner's Grail mysticism is reflected in the chaotic drawing *Faiths in Decline* (Plate 10). Reading from bottom to top, and from right to left, we see humanity sinking down into the sea of life, with the bayonets symbolizing the authority of the state, exerted by force. The Serpent has seized mankind in its treacherous stranglehold, but rescue is at hand in the form of a figure who, with her eyes closed and a halo about her head, comes floating along on two swans across the whole surface of the drawing (an echo of Wagner's *Lohengrin*). This is Mysticism, the personification of Toorop's belief in a better world.

Towards the end of the century his belief takes on increasingly powerful forms and finds expression in his drawings of human heads, portrayed from life; in *The Sower*, for instance, Toorop's wife appears twice, full-face and in profile (Plate 9). Generally, the heads are shown with lifted faces and closed eyes, as if they were going aloft to a better world (Plate 12b). In 1905 Toorop's questing spirit, after his conversion to Roman Catholicism, found tranquillity. This is apparent in his new style: in *Procession of Souls beside the Ocean* (Plate 11), the delicately drawn heads of the baby and the young and the old woman – symbol of Woman's course through life – are all of them true to life, without any distortion.

Johan Thorn Prikker (1868–1932)
Johan Thorn Prikker, Toorop's junior by ten years, completed a course of study at the Hague Academy of Fine Arts. For a short while he painted impressionistic urban scenes after the manner of Breitner, but soon he switched over to symbolism. However, he lacked the support of the literary world, especially that of the influential art critic J. P. Veth, who was always defending Toorop, Derkinderen and Roland Holst. Prikker was the target for a great deal of intrigue and obstruction on the part of the older generation that set the fashion in *Pulchri Studio* and the *Haagse Kunstkring*. In Holland he always remained a misunderstood and neglected artist. Only H. P. Bremmer, the art educationalist, and W. J. H. Leuring, a doctor from Scheveningen, appreciated his work, and the latter proved to be a true Maecenas.
It was not until 1904 that he found in Germany more sympathy for his creative talent as a craftsman. The same was the case with Henry van de Velde, whose acquaintance Prikker made in 1893, when he became a member of the *Société des XX* in Brussels, and in whose house in Uccle he made his first batik and stained-glass designs.
Van de Velde's style, as it was in about 1893, with its striking ornamentation of parallel lines, inspired Prikker's symbolist compositions (Plate 16). How he composed is revealed in his letters to the writer Henri Borel, who at the time was in China and the Dutch East Indies. Written between 1892 and 1897, in the difficult years of financial worry and neglect, these letters served as a safety valve for his troubled existence. These letters, with drawings in the text, make his basic intention clear: he does not want to fix the visual impression of the outer world, but the *essence* of things contained in general abstract concepts such as life, purity, mysticism, but also in the emotions of love, hate, depression. And a single person or object could symbolize the idea. The head of a young girl symbolizes spring, a large hand holding flowers is the sower (Plate 14b).
Whereas Toorop imparted action to his symbols, in Prikker's work all is tranquillity and serenity. Here too space disappears. The lines take on an independent function. Drawn in thick or thin loops, they indicate – like a crescendo or pianissimo in music – what should be stressed and what should not. In *The Bride* (Plate IV) the accent falls on love (the bride herself): she is no more than a thin veil, which is closely connected with suffering (Christ).

The connection is shown by the myrtle branch that gradually turns into Christ's crown of thorns. Misery is already lying in wait for young love; it will be ensnared by treacherous sensuality in the shape of the phallic tulips and the skull-like snapdragons. The dull purples and greens of this pointillist painting, together with its lines, symbolize mildness and tenderness. Thorn Prikker found inspiration in the Japanese prints of Utamaro and Hokusai, and in the photos of Old Chinese works of art which Borel sent to him, but nature itself fascinated him no less. In his drawings, rugged rock formations seen in the Ardennes and gnarled tree trunks change into figures that might be cut from roughly grained wood: monks wrestling in solitude with the petty-minded world, clinging with confidence to the Cross of Christ (Plate 17). In these monastic images – the theme was taken from a poem by Emile Verhaeren – and in the Saviour on the Cross that he did for a poster (Plate 15) Prikker gave vent to the emotions inherent in his lonely struggle against mediocre talents and the hypocrisy of society.

Antoon Derkinderen (1859–1925)

Derkinderen was with Toorop at the Brussels Academy of Fine Arts in 1882. For a short time afterwards his paintings were in the manner of the Hague School with its clear, precise brushwork. He cannot really be termed an impressionist. To quote Henriëtte Roland Holst, the poet and wife of R. N. Roland Holst, he had a character 'from which impressionism rolled off like drops of water from the surface of polished marble'. After an inward development which made him realize that it is the artist's duty to serve the community, and that he must aim at unifying architecture and painting, Derkinderen carried out two official commissions in accordance with this ideal. As a result, these two murals (oil paintings on canvas pasted onto the wall), the *Procession* for the Beguinage Church in Amsterdam and the *Eerste Bossche Wand* in the Town Hall of 's-Hertogenbosch, show a certain nebulosity of colour and blurring of images. The fact was that Derkinderen thought these 'mural' colours (vague, grey tones) to be in accord with the building, i.e. the wall, with which the painting had to form a unity. His patrons, to whom this kind of conception was quite foreign, consequently refused to accept his creations – in the beginning. Their objections – like those of their contemporaries – were directed not towards the content but towards the style. The attenuated, subdued colours were regarded as 'faded'. Derkinderen's work was indeed stylized, but it was hardly distorted at all. The visionary unity of painting and architecture was realized neither in the *Eerste Bossche Wand*, a mural in which the communal ideal of the Catholic Middle Ages is symbolized in scenes from the

Crusades, nor in the *Tweede Bossche Wand* (a second mural, dating from 1896), in which the cathedral of 's-Hertogenbosch and the theme of Labour are pictured, now in bright, sharply outlined colours. But Derkinderen *did* achieve unity in his book decorations. Here he did pioneering work that had great influence on younger illustrators and illuminators. In the volume issued in 1893 to commemorate the previous year's Exhibition of Contemporary Dutch Painting (Plate 18) and in the *de luxe* edition of the drama *Gysbreght van Aemstel* by the Dutch seventeenth-century poet Joost van den Vondel, the illustrations accompanying the text and the typeface itself with its decorative characters are in one and the same style, following the example of William Morris and also under the influence of Walter Crane. The flaming torch brandished over Amsterdam by the evil termagant, symbol of fate and destruction, is drawn with the same twisting lines that are characteristic of Crane's illustrations (Plate 19).

Another fine example of symbolism is the frontispiece to the printed edition of Alphons Diepenbrock's *Missa* (Plate 20). The harp between the censers is meant to suggest the nature of the music. The same symbols are to be found again in the work of Melchior Lechter, the German artist who illustrated Stefan George's *Die Lieder von Traum und Tod*, with the ominously mysterious pair of hands playing the harp and surrounded by swirling clouds of incense (Plate 21).

Of great importance to the realization of his ideals was Derkinderen's friendship with his fellow Roman Catholic, the composer Alphons Diepenbrock, and also the support he got from the painter-critic J. P. Veth, who in his instructive writings never failed to defend Derkinderen against the attacks of general criticism.

Richard Nicolaüs Roland Holst (1868–1938)
Roland Holst started his artistic career at the State Academy of Fine Arts in Amsterdam when August Allebé was director.

In 1890, after his academic studies, he came under the influence of the impressionist Breitner. But it was not long before, with his speculative turn of mind, he turned away from impressionism. Thought came first for Roland Holst: it was the sum of his existence, his philosophy of life. Observable reality occupied second place only. This set him apart from the impressionists, who were never sated with the abundance of visual sensations. Roland Holst's symbolism, only short-lived, must be considered a period of preparation for his monumental works of the twentieth century (murals in the Amsterdam Stock Exchange, designs for stained-glass windows, and so on). During and after the First World War Roland Holst exercised, especially in his position as director of the State Academy of Fine Arts, a strong influence on the younger generation of artists. His strong point was his essays – articles on art and artists – and not his pictorial work.

In the drawings and lithographs belonging to his symbolist period from 1891 to 1895, concern for perspective has certainly decreased, though not to such an extent that the flat surface – later to be declared by Roland Holst to be the beginning and end of decorative art – alone remains. There is no distortion to speak of.

Of the symbolists, Roland Holst had the most intensive contacts with Dutch literary circles; this was due to his friendship with Albert Verwey and Veth, his marriage to Henriëtte van der Schalk, and his acquaintance with Frederik van Eeden, Herman Gorter and André Jolles. He also kept in touch with the Belgian artists of the *Société des XX* – though not to the same extent as Jan Toorop – especially with George Lemmen and Henry van de Velde. Lemmen's influence can be detected in the cover of the catalogue of the 1892 Exhibition of Contemporary Dutch Painting (Plate 23), on which the letters have the same spiky, thorny shape as those used by Lemmen in his illustrations for the periodical *L'Art moderne* (Plate 22). They both show Woman as the symbol of this new art, with the disk of the sun of idealism shining in the distance.

For a very short while Roland Holst succumbed to the charm of Sar Péladan during the latter's visit to Holland, but a much more lasting and profound influence was Vincent van Gogh. In December 1892 Roland Holst organized an exhibition of van Gogh's work and designed the cover of the catalogue (Plate 24). This time the setting sun is on the horizon: this, like the withered sunflower - van Gogh's favourite flower - represents the extinguished life of the painter, who at the time was practically unknown in the Netherlands. The aureole round the sunflower proves that this is not a flower chosen at random: it is meant to radiate a sacred devotion. Perhaps this is an expression of reverence for the artist whose life ended so tragically. The motif is adopted from Rossetti's *Beata Beatrix* (Plate 12a) – at the hour of her death Dante's beloved receives a poppy from a bird wearing an aureole as the messenger of death.

It was under the inspiration of van Gogh's reed-pen drawings with their parallel lines and suns (with van Gogh the expression of a fierce passion for life, with Roland Holst merely background decoration) that Roland Holst drew the gloomy sky in his lithograph *Anangkè* (Plate 25). Here the symbol of Fate (the Greek word is taken from the poem of the same name by Albert Verwey) and of Roland Holst's melancholy is the cadaverous head of Prometheus. Greek mythology tells us that Prometheus was punished by Zeus for daring to show mortals how to make fire. Chained to Mount Caucasus, he was helpless to defend himself against the three-headed eagle devouring his liver by day, which was restored in each succeeding night.

The influence of the Pre-Raphaelite Dante Gabriel Rossetti, on whom Roland Holst published an essay, emerged clearly in the years after 1893. Just as the Pre-Raphaelites clothed their personal emotions in scenes from myths and fairy tales, so Roland Holst symbolized his own melancholy mood in the figure of a Maltese Knight, *Un beau sire grave* (Plate 27). The medieval attire of this earnest young man is, like the fence, drawn in the manner of Rossetti (Plate 26). The *beau sire* of the title is probably taken from Péladan's most famous book *Le vice suprême* (1884), in which a Maltese Knight also makes his appearance as the self-portrait of the pure Péladan.

Peasant girls from the old moorland village of Laren, studied from the life, occasionally appear in the lithographs as symbols of female innocence, sometimes with their attributes the rose and the sunflower (Plate 29b). There is evidence of a stylistic influence derived from illustrations by Aubrey Beardsley (Plate 29a), but the truly formative influence on Roland Holst's style after 1900 was his journey to London in the winter of 1893–94, when he paid a visit to the book illuminators Charles Ricketts and Charles Shannon. The typography which they designed can be seen again in the decoration of the first edition of Henriëtte van der Schalk's *Sonnetten en Verzen in Terzinen geschreven* (Sonnets and Stanzas written in Tercets).

These four representatives of symbolism in Dutch art had been led to symbolism by their mental disposition. In their best years there was occasionally something of the seer in them. They were musical, appreciative of literature, and of a philosophic and religious turn of mind. As they wanted to depict more than visible reality, their symbolist work was in sharp contrast with the pictures of their contemporaries Breitner and Isaac Israels, who had never felt the need to reveal their ideas in their work but were content to experience reality as an aesthetic sensation. As a result there never was a period in which the discontinuity of styles was so clear-cut as in the years of the *fin de siècle*. At one and the same time the work of painters of the same generation showed such trends as impressionism, expressionism, an inchoate cubism and Art Nouveau.

The symbolist period of the four Dutchmen was an intermediate phase of preparation for their creative years after the turn of the century, when they were to realize their destiny and find recognition.

1965

Bibliography

General
Jan Veth, *Hollandsche Teekenaars van dezen tijd*, Amsterdam, 1905.
Aeg. W. Timmerman, *Tim's Herinneringen*, Amsterdam, 1938.
A. M. Hammacher, *Symbolisme en Abstractie in De Groene Amsterdammer 75 jaar*, 1951, pp. 104–5.
Bettina Polak, *Het fin-de-siècle in de Nederlandse schilderkunst. De Symbolistische Beweging 1890–1900*, The Hague, 1955.
Gerard Brom, *Schilderkunst en literatuur in de 19e eeuw*, Utrecht, 1959 (Aula Books).
Kunstenaarslevens: Albert Verwey's Correspondence with Alphons Diepenbrock, Herman Gorter, R. N. Roland Holst, Henriëtte van der Schalk and J. Th. Toorop, edited by Dr Mea Nijland (née Verwey), Assen, 1959 (Van Gorcum).

On Jan Toorop
Miek Janssen, *Schets over het leven en enkele werken van Jan Toorop*, Amsterdam, 1920.
A. Plasschaert, *Jan Toorop*, Amsterdam, 1925.
J. B. Knipping, *Jan Toorop*, Amsterdam, 1947 (Palet Series).

On Johan Thorn Prikker
Brieven. The authentic letters are in the possession of the Literary Museum, The Hague.
Brieven van Johan Thorn Prikker, with a preface by Henri Borel, Amsterdam, 1897.
August Hoff, *Johan Thorn Prikker*, Recklinghausen, 1958 (Verlag Aurel Bongers, Monographien zur rheinisch-westfälischen Kunst der Gegenwart, Band 12).

On Antoon Derkinderen
A. M. Hammacher, *De levenstijd van Antoon Der Kinderen*, Amsterdam, 1932.

On R. N. Roland Holst
Henriëtte Roland Holst, *Kinderjaren en jeugd van R. N. Roland Holst*, Zeist, 1940.
Henriëtte Roland Holst, *Het vuur brandde voort. Levensherinneringen*, Amsterdam, 1949.

I   Toorop ±1890

II   Toorop ± 1891

IV   Thorn Prikker 1893

1   Toorop 1892

3   Toorop 1892

4   Toorop 1899

5   Toorop 1892–1897

7   **Toorop 1893**

9   Toorop ±1895

10 **Toorop 1894**

11   Toorop ±1900

a

b

12a   **D. G. Rossetti ±1863**
12b   **Toorop 1897**

ARBEID
VOOR DE VROUW

13   Toorop 1898

a

b

14a   Roland Holst 1893
14b   Thorn Prikker 1893

REVUE BIMESTRIELLE POUR L'ART APPLIQUÉ
EDITEUR IMPRIMEUR
H. KLEINMANN ET Cie KENAUPARK 9. HARLEM, HOLLANDE.
PRIX 45 FRANCS PAR AN .15 ESTAMPES LA LIVRAISON.

J THORN PRIKKER.

15 **Thorn Prikker** ±1896

16   Henry van de Velde ±1893

17   Thorn Prikker 1894

18   Derkinderen ±1892

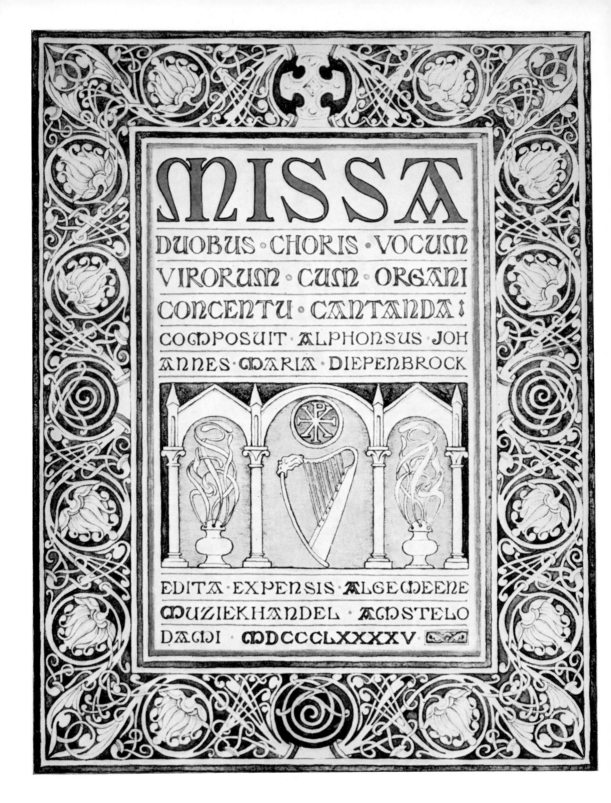

MISSA
DUOBUS · CHORIS · VOCUM
VIRORUM · CUM · ORGANI
CONCENTU · CANTANDA :
COMPOSUIT · ALPHONSUS · JOH
ANNES · MARIA · DIEPENBROCK

EDITA · EXPENSIS · ALGEMEENE
MUZIEKHANDEL · AMSTELO
DAMI · MDCCCLXXXXV

DIE LIE-DER
VON TRA-UM
UND TOD

1899

21   Melchior Lechter 1899

22   George Lemmen 1892

23   Roland Holst 1892

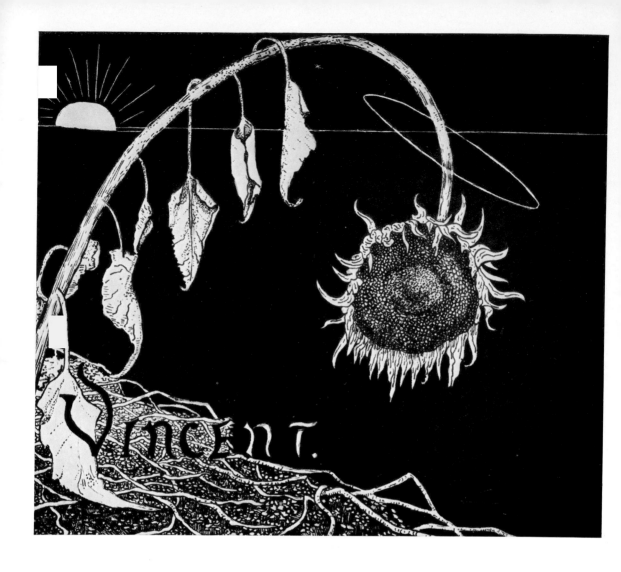

24   **Roland Holst 1892**

26   **D. G. Rossetti 1868**

27   **Roland Holst 1893**

28   Roland Holst 1894

a

b

29a   **Aubrey Beardsley 1893**
29b   **Roland Holst 1895**

31   Henricus 1894

32   **De Nerée tot Babberich 1901**